mary was here

an effigy of sorts

Copyright © 2024 Mary Simmerling
Original edition copyright © 2005

ALL RIGHTS RESERVED. No part of this publication may be reproduced, stored in a retrieval system, or transmitted in any form or by any process – electronic, mechanical, photocopying, recording, or otherwise – without the prior written permission of the copyright owner and Write Where We Belong Press. The scanning, uploading and distribution of this via the internet or any other means without the permission of the publisher is illegal and punishable by law. Please purchase only authorized electronic editions, and do not participate in or encourage electronic piracy of copyrighted materials. Your support of the author's rights is appreciated.

Published by:
Write Where We Belong Press
October 10, 2024

Cover photo by Charles Deluvio, Unsplash
Cover design & layout by Sarah Pierson

ISBN 978-1-0688285-2-2 ppbk
ISBN 978-1-0688285-3-9 ebook

Printed and bound in Canada by Hume Media Inc.

for Thomas, breath of my breath—
without you this would not have been possible.

"And when we speak we are afraid our words will not be heard nor welcomed. But when we are silent, we are still afraid. So it is better to speak."

— Audre Lorde

author's note

In 2005 as I was preparing to write my Ph.D. dissertation on autonomy and its limits in the context of living organ donation, I found myself instead writing a collection of poems about the challenges I faced navigating the world after I was sexually assaulted. In my dissertation I was arguing that justice is the single most important moral principle, and that without it autonomy is not possible. The poems in this collection emerged from the intersection of the personal and the theoretical; from places where autonomy is often violated, and justice feels elusive but desperately necessary.

I've decided to publish this collection now, almost 20 years later, in its original form, because the rawness and urgency of the words still resonate deeply with me. And I now know that they represent not only my experience, but give voice to the experiences of other survivors. One of the pieces – "what i was wearing" – inspired a global social justice movement in protest against a world that too often accepts sexual violence as inevitable or normative and seeks to blame victims rather than perpetrators. Many of the poems in this collection reveal the insidious ways in which the ordinary happenings of life are upended for survivors of sexual violence – things like listening to the news, going to the movies, attending a party, or simply going for a run. Focusing in on these seemingly mundane moments serves to magnify the ways in which the implicit endorsement of violence against women remains disturbingly normative and pervasive in society and globally. As I wrote in "not guilty," the cultural endorsement of violence against women is a special kind of insanity that blinds us incompletely to what is happening around us every day.

As I write this note, I am reminded that just last month the Taliban passed a law prohibiting women from speaking in public, based on the claim that our very voices are intimate and should not be heard outside the home. This latest human rights violation is on top of the already existing laws that prohibit women in some parts of the world from showing our faces in public, and women and girls from going to school or pursuing work outside the home. Under the Taliban's rule, women are also prevented from serving as lawyers or judges, effectively cutting off the very ability to fight these inhumane laws.

The truth is that the power of our voices is terrifying to those who seek to oppress us. Our voices are so dangerous to their objectives that they prefer to silence us altogether. But for today, I still have a voice. In the pages that follow, I share with you my intimate voice and stories, and hope that in so doing there will be more space for others to share theirs as well.

Mary Simmerling
Ottawa, Ontario

poems in effigy (in six parts)

prologue	1
in my dream	3
part 1: mary, rarefied	5
missing	7
crime scene	8
what i was wearing	10
erase	13
part 2: struggling, alone with me	17
holy	19
silently	21
the way the evening ends	23
what i meant to say is	24
over now	26
part 3: secrets of survival	31
backward land	33
part 4: the social animal	35
pretty	37
in my car	38
branded	39
monster	41
hazing	42
american dream	45
in the gym	46
labels	48

not guilty	50
part 5: learning to breathe, and speak	53
in my body	55
in the kitchen	58
part 6: how to change the world	63
grammar lessons	65
thought experiment	67
epilogue	71
meltdown	73

prologue

in my dream

there is a note
inscribed on vapors
in invisible ink.

it is hard
to see
this secret message

floating
as it is
among the ethers.

dear mary
where are you?
love, god.

mary, rarefied

missing

physical description
sex: female
height: 5'6"
weight: 110
hair: blonde
eyes: blue
other physical characteristics: lithe and beautiful traits and
habits: has been known to read and exercise

age at disappearance: 18
age now: unchanged
    (it's possible everything's been frozen in time, you see)

last seen: los angeles, california, july 4, 1987, late late at night
    (just barely july 5)
possible locations: may have gone underground

please contact:
mary, owner of said body.

crime scene

this is what we do:
we mark it off with
yellow tape
DANGER POLICE
CRIME SCENE
GET BACK
STAY AWAY
CRIME SCENE
DANGER KEEP
OUT.

and then when
it's over
we tear it down.

since
(after all)
no one lives there
anymore

who would
live there

who could
live there

after what happened.

tear it down.

no one l
lives there
anymore.

this is what i did:
i put my clothes
back on
my body
after he was done with me
and then
i left.

(that is
i have been trying
to leave
but i am stuck here
won't anyone help me
tear it down.)

GET BACK
STAY AWAY
CRIME SCENE
DANGER
KEEP OUT.

what i was wearing

was this:
from the top a
white t-shirt
cotton
short-sleeved
and round at the neck

this was tucked into a
jean skirt
(also cotton)
ending just above the knees
and belted at the top

underneath all this was a
white cotton bra and
white underpants
(though probably not a set)

on my feet
white tennis shoes
the kind one plays tennis in

and then finally
silver earrings, and lip gloss.

this is what i was wearing
that day
that night
that fourth of july
in 1987.

you may be wondering
why this matters
or even how i remember
every item
in such detail

you see
i have been asked this question
many times
it has been called to my mind
many times
this question this
answer these
details.

but my answer much
awaited much
anticipated seems flat
somehow
given the rest of the details of
that night
during which
at some point i
was raped.

and i wonder
what answer
what details
would give comfort
could give comfort
to you
my questioners

seeking comfort where
there is
alas
no comfort
to be found.

if only it were so simple
if only we could
end rape
by simply changing clothes.

i remember also what
he was wearing that
night
even though
it's true
that no one has
ever asked.

erase

he called me the
next day.

she must have told him
what i said.
that morning in
her car driving
home.

she must have given him
my number
so he could call me
clear things up.

(silly girl.)

i heard his voice
pronounce my name.

glibly.
smugly.

he said
would you like to go to dinner.

as if it were
ok.

as if he had not
done what he did do.

as if i was
confused
mistaken.
able to eat.

as if i would
acquiesce.
as if i had done so
already.

as if it were
ok.

what he did
to me.

as if i did not have bruises
on my body.
as if he had not put them there.

as if i could speak.
eat.
sleep.
dress myself.
leave home.

breathe.
live.

he said
would you like to go to dinner.

as if i was not reliving it
again.
still
living it.

as if
i had perhaps enjoyed it.

as if i could not
even trust

my own memory my
own judgment my
own experience.
as if he could take that from me too. and
i
i said no.
again.

struggling, alone with me

holy

people sometimes say it
must be so special for
you
now
after what happened. it
must be
so special
holy almost.

and the truth
is
the truth is
that it is
holy almost
sort of.

let me explain.

this is what happens:
first, i leave
my body
behind
(under
astray
away)
i go
away.

and yet
there i am i
am there.
and yet
i am not.

my body
before and
after and
me
trying to find my way back.

body
and spirit
divided and
yet still one
somehow.
sometimes.

holy
sort of.

holes inside me
holes in my head
my body
so many holes
in my life
afterwards.

silently

he said
it is like you are exercising.
pushing through the last mile

it is as if
you are
in a trance
seeing nothing

as if
you are not
even there.

he said
i don't know why
you do this
to me.

he said
i love
you
i love you.

and i said
i cannot find
my way back
to you

i am lost here
among the ruins

i said

i don't understand
why you want to be there

where i cannot see
cannot be.

except that i
did not say
it aloud.
but only to
myself.

the way the evening ends

i think
he is going
to cry.

if only
i could
also.

this is the way the
evening ends.

what i meant to say is

this:
it is lonely here
inside of me
and i am frightened.

i feel sometimes
as though i am living

in an abandoned building
windowless
cold
stark
dirty
and dark.

living here
(yes, here)
among the ruins of
what was

living here among
the traces of
squatters
long gone.

i wanted
to tell you

it is lonely here
inside of me.

i think
always

sometimes
maybe
it will go away
(please god, make it go away).

this
is what i meant to say:
i want
to come back
it is lonely here
inside of me this
way.

this is what i meant
to say
when i looked at you
but did not speak.

over now

people sometimes ask:
will you ever
get over it?

it is not so much that
they are waiting for
this

for me
to get over
it

(how long ago
did it happen
now?)

it is rather that
they want to
believe
that they have to believe
(please god let it be true)
that one can
get over
it

just in case
it should happen
 to them
(please god let it be over now)

just in case
it should happen
to their daughter

their partner their
wife
their mother
sister brother
friend
child

just in case it should happen to
them
(please god let it be over)
they ask
because they want to believe
that one can
get over it
(please god let it be true)
striking so randomly
as it does

any time
(day or night)

anywhere (in
the alley on
the train
at the bus stop

in the stairway
the bedroom the
hallway)

without the least discrimination
(black white yellow brown
young old
man woman)
caring about nothing

relentlessly devouring
everything in its wake
(please god let it be over now)
they ask because
they want to believe
they have to believe
(please god let it be true)
that one can
get over
being raped.

(please god let it be true.)

secrets of survival

backward land

this was my daily ritual: first
i would unwrap
a fresh bar of soap
grab a new razor & shaving cream
fresh washcloth,
toothbrush and paste,
and shampoo and conditioner

all this i would take
into the shower
scrubbing my skin, hair, and teeth
clean

after which i'd towel dry
and then
pull on fresh underwear, a
t-shirt and shorts
some socks and running shoes.

then i'd grab my dog
and my phone
and head for the door

which i would not go through
but simply check
to be sure
it was locked.

this is what i would do
each night
before pulling back the sheets to
go to bed.

the social animal

pretty

he smiled
and said

you look so pretty
when you cry.

in my car

the news reporter said
in a calm voice
as if she were reading the weather

she said
last night
an eight year old girl was raped.

and then in the same breath
(and without hesitation)
she said—
she was not seriously injured.

and i
i pulled off to the side of the road
and i cried.

for the girl
and for the reporter.

branded

we locked eyes
for just
a moment.

both sets
downcast.

at the end of 5 miles
i was already sweating.

still i felt
a prick
the wave of adrenaline
rush.

(eyes darting around)

he turned the corner
and looked back
slowly

with his whole body
he took me in.

(and i wondered all at once
was it too long
his glance back at me?
was i overheated from the run
or was it too hot for the coat he was wearing?
was he
out for a coffee
or at home on the street?
how fast could my legs go
if i had to get away?
why hadn't i eaten more?

brought my dog?)
(eyes darting around)
i looked back too
and saw
another stranger this
one walking tall
smiling
talking into the air on his phone.

and i felt
my heart
slowing down.

my body slowing
down.

my pace
almost a walk now.

and then
i could see them both
equidistant from me.

both holding me
in their gaze.

and i
i looked at them
and i wondered
(silently, ashamedly)
whether it was just his
whiteness
(falsely, arbitrarily)
reassuring me
after all.

monster

in the theatre they
did not miss
one handful of popcorn
as they watched him

(projected all in widescreen
with full dolby surround)

repeatedly rape her
first with his own body
and then again
with a steel pipe.

hazing

i found out about it
later.

about how
they were supposed to
record everything.

they listened to it
anyway.

they listened to his
date with me.

crowded around the recorder
they listened
as i broke down.

they listened to me cry
when he tried to kiss me.

they listened to me make
tearful apologies.

they listened to me
try to explain
what had happened that
i had been raped a few
months before.

they listened to me
chokingly mutter
that i was sorry.

for thinking i was ready to date
for ruining his night.

i found out later
that some of them laughed as
they listened to me.
as they listened
to our date.

at the end of which
he was supposed to have sex with me
and surreptitiously record it for
them all to enjoy.
a task they had all been given
a way to prove their worthiness
of brotherhood.

still
they listened.

crowded around the recorder in
the basement
of the fraternity house.

they listened to me
and they did not get up.

they did not run from the room.
they did not say turn it off.
they did not scream out i
can't listen to this
i can't bear to listen to this.

they listened to me
and they did not cry.

they did not grab the recorder
and smash it against the wall.

they did not pound their strong fists on the floor. they
did not scream out
what is happening to us
what have we become.

i found out later
that some of them apologized to
him for me
for what an awful date i was.

but none of them ever apologized to me even
though
it's true they
saw me
every day.

american dream

she said
(incredulously)
you're so pretty
you don't even need
to go
to school
(what a waste).

he said
(longingly)
you're so smart
(makes me want to fuck you)
i'd love to
read your work.

in the gym

the good guy said to me
tell them
that you made him
do it to you.

tell them
you made him
do it
to you

and he smiled.
and i
i stood there in
front of him

my face
scraped up
my shoulder
cloaked in a fresh scab
my knee
bruised and torn.

he had asked what happened
concerned look on his face.

and i said

i fell off my bike
a few days ago
head first
over the handlebars.

that's when
he smiled
and said

tell them
that you made him
do it to you.

and i
i stood there in
front of him
and i realized
he was flirting with me.

labels

they took magic markers
and wrote on her naked body.

she did not flinch
or laugh even
at the pressure of the markers.

it did not tickle her
the letters turning into words
all across her naked body.

S-L-U-T
sketched out across her arm.

W-H-O-R-E
trailing down the length of her abdomen.

it's true that the writing
did not disturb her then
passed out as she had been for hours

when they took up the magic markers
and wrote on her naked body
after they had finished with her.

perhaps they thought—
if only they could convince themselves
she was really just
a whore after all
(*what a stupid slut*)
they could make everyone else
believe it too.

perhaps that's why
they videotaped
the whole thing.
so everyone could see
she'd asked for it
provoked them to do it
she'd wanted it

(just like the girls
on the videotapes
for sale in all the stores.).

that she'd consented
to the whole thing
(*no, no- that is, she did before, yes*)
just before
she passed out.

not guilty

said the jury
of his peers.

(he had his back to us
and then there was the
grainy tape
poor quality
home video)

not guilt—
they said

(you see we could not be sure
what he was doing
with his penis
up there by her mouth
perhaps he was trying to
help her
she was unconscious
after all)

(won't someone please help her)
not guilty
said the jury

(having turned their faces away so
awful were
the acts
captured on
the tape
who could stand to watch)

not guilty
they said
(by reason of
cultural endorsement a
special kind
of insanity that
blinds you
incompletely)

not guilty

(you see this one
he had sex with her earlier
behind a locked door
he said
she liked it

no, no—
we have no tape
of that
though)

after which
she began to shake
uncontrollably

(it was the other two
who were doing her
on the tape
no they're not on trial here)

(no, no-
they've fled the country)

(this one —
he was just standing there
watching perhaps)

as she shook
uncontrollably
when the verdict was read

(won't someone please help her)

not guilty
they said

(and snuck out the back door).

learning to breathe, and speak

in my body

i could feel

my breath

the air
rushing in
and out
of my lungs
steadily
rhythmically

beads of sweat
lining up
all along my skin
trickling down my
face

my heart

pumping blood
working
to send signals
to send life
throughout my
arms
my legs
my back

my body

i could feel

and for a moment
i thought

perhaps
i will fly away

take these legs
and soar
up into the ethers

give snowflakes a home
inside my mouth
all along the way

raise my arms up
over my head
rejoice

at last
i could feel
my body

as i watched the miles
go by
underfoot

running
so effortlessly now

as if i was just
another part of
the air

i could feel
my breath

and i realized
finally
(at least for this moment)
i had come home.

in the kitchen

everyone could hear him
holding court
with his friends

close to the refrigerator
and the booze

i watched
as he
threw his head back
laughing heartily into
the crowd
(all charm now)
i listened to him
recount
what had happened
the night before

smiling
he said:
man, she was hot–
she was so drunk
no, no–
her friend took her home
(*that bitch*)
whisked her away right
out of my arms

(palms turned up, shoulders shrugging)
yeah, I made out with her

no, no—
after she threw up
(aren't you listening at all?)

just before she passed out

yeah, i made out with her
just before she left—
(swigging his drink)

man, she was hot
(leaning back now,
head cocked to the side)

everyone got a piece of her
she gave mark a blow job
(*lucky bastard*)

(everyone laughing now)
(everyone except me)

he came in her mouth
just before she threw up.

yeah, i made out
with her
(leaning in now, all confidence and charm)
just before she left.

and suddenly
i could feel
my feet moving
rushing towards him
just a few steps

and there i was
in his crowd

and he was smiling.
looking at me

everyone looking at me now—

taking me full in
with their eyes

(who brought the blonde)

(maybe she wants some too)

and i stuck my hand out and
i said:

i want to congratulate you
for being so brave
to tell your story here
in this kitchen
in front of all of us
so confidently
so honestly
so loudly
so that we might all hear
so that we would not miss
a single word.

i said:
i do not know
many men

who would so boldly confess
to having done
what you did.

and i want to know more.

i want to know this:
could you taste his come
in her mouth
when you kissed her—
or was it all just
so much throw up by then?
tell me:
what was it like?

and i stood there
in front of him
and i waited
for an answer.

i did not throw my head back
and i did not laugh heartily
into the crowd.

i stood there in
front of him
and i listened
to the raw silence created
by my own voice.

how to change the world

grammar lessons

she
wanted it
was asking for it

(did you see
what she was wearing)

had it coming
to her

(did you see
how she was walking
out alone
after dark)

deserved what she got—
raped.

choose rape.
the grammar just
won't allow it.

even if
we do.

even if
we cannot

stop
thinking this way.

our very language
rejects
this distortion.

cannot accommodate
this conception
of rape.

she
wanted it
was asking for it

(did you see
the purple bruises
in the shape of his hands
all along
her lovely neck)

had it coming
to her—

(did you see
the way she walked
afterwards
hunched over
a posthumous attempt to
protect her insides)

deserved
what
she got

(did you see
her eyes
like vacant pools
i wonder did she drown
in all those tears).

thought experiment

try this:

imagine
a world
where rape
was as despised
as deplorable
contemptible
unacceptable
as morally reprehensible as
lynching.

imagine
a day
where violence
against women
was repugnant
rather than
ordinary

was tragic
catastrophic
and heartbreaking
rather than
entertaining.

where women were
no longer bought
and sold
like so much chattel.

were no longer
just
so many rented holes.

and now:
try it at home.

try it in the morning
over coffee
with toast.

try it at the office
in the boardroom
the classroom.

try it in the emergency room
and the courtroom.

try it in the nightclub
try in the bathroom and
the coatroom.

try it at the bar
and the table.
try it over dessert.

try it
in the evening
before bed
with your partner
your spouse
your children
and grandchildren.

try it on the bus
 the train
the plane.
try it in the alley.
try it in your car.

try it in the gym on
the playground the
football field
the basketball court.

try it at church.

try it everywhere
the implicit endorsement of
violence against women is
allowed to lurk.

epilogue

meltdown

rape brings devastation
it can turn a life
into an ashen existence
leaving things frozen
as they were.

still—
the body persists somehow
wishing eventually
to erupt
destroy
make anew
offer some hope of release
escape
from the memories
mental etchings carved
out of flesh invisible to
other eyes.

if only it were just a nightmare
after all.

but it is real and
i wonder:

what would it be like
if the devastation were visible
on the outside
like tidal waves
tornadoes
volcanoes.

i wonder would they still ask
what were you wearing?

www.ingramcontent.com/pod-product-compliance
Lightning Source LLC
Chambersburg PA
CBHW070438010526
44118CB00014B/2104